WARMTH AND LIGHT ARE WITH US ALWAYS

Nihil was born at sea. Her mother died in childbirth. Neither Nihil nor her mother, Ruonob, had a home nation. Nihil's mother had lived on a remote, unnamed, island. Everyone on the island lived simply. They fed themselves from fruit of the island's trees, seeds they had planted and fish from the waters surrounding the island.

A small boat was shipwrecked on the island. One of the persons on the ship became intimate with Ruonob. They conceived Nihil. The men also found oil on the island. Soon the island was invaded by men from a neighboring island who came to extract the oil. Nihil's father did not realize he was now a father. He sailed to other islands to deliver oil.

The ecology of the island was devastated by the search for oil. Ruonob was unable to feed herself or her child. One of the men from the shipwrecked boat returned to the island to check on the progress of oil extraction. He recognized Ruonob. She told him about Nihil and her search for Nihil's father. He took Ruonob to the oil island to find Nihil's father.

The father was not there. Ruonob began a long search on the sea to find Nihil's father. During that search Nihil was born. The boatman took Nihil and her mother to a nearby island. A missionary on the island assisted Ruonob in her death. Her final wish was that Nihil return to the island where she had been conceived. The missionary agreed to do that.

The missionary was transferred before he was able to bring Nihil to her mother's home. So Nihil had to visit Alaska, London, the island she was raised the,.... first few years of her life. Eventually she found her father on the oil island where her father had gone after her conception. Nihil and her father (James) went to the island where she was conceived.

When they reached the island it had not yet recovered from the damage created by the oil searchers. James had brought some equipment and had some knowledge of how to correct some of the effects of the oil production. His work with the oil island had been limited to transporting oil ready to be shipped so he had little experience correcting oil damage to the island. Some of the problems created by oil production neither he nor the natives coul correct.

They tried to clean up water of the stream running through the island and water of the surrounding sea. They lacked the knowledge or the equipment to solve this problem. Islanders were ingenious enough to live as best they could despite problems caused by the presence of oil.

Nihil and James quickly adapted to the language and culture or life of the persons and customs on the island. They quickly became involved in the activity of the community. They frequently visited the stones placed on the island to commemorate events of Nihil's life.

The place they liked most was the spot where Nihil was conceived. They spent much time there. The spot brought back fond memories for James. He could almost see Ruonob. Even though James only vaguely remembers her, this spot sparks his memory. He remembers her beauty, her simplicity, the gentleness of her voice, her smile, the twinkle in her eyes, all the qualities that attracted him. .

As he looked at Nihil, James saw so many of those same characteristics. James grasped Nihil and held her close to himself. It was such a firm grasp, it startled Nihil. James realized Nihil did not have the same memory of this spot as he did. But Nihil began to react the same way as James did each time she visited the spot.

After several visits Nihil always had the same sensation. She began to notice James' strong reactions at the spot. Previously when they left the spot, reactions seemed to cease in both of them. Nihil became curious and began to wonder what was happening to her and her father.

Nihil asked James what was happening. He told Nihil: "It's your mother's spirit. Even though her body dies, her spirit is still alive. That spirit remains strong especially when her spirit senses our presence." Nihil and James continued their walk. They remained silent, each reflecting on the meaning of their common experience.

After a few minutes Nihil said: "I remember having this same feeling and experience when I visited my mother's grave." James replied: "Our spirits are not bound by the same restrictions as our bodies. Our spirit is present in many different places at the same time. We need to be sensitive to that presence."

The sense of the presence of the spirit excited Nihil. She spoke to James: "So you bringing me here helps me to make my mother's presence more real." James had not thought of that, but he was so excited with his daughter's wisdom he began to cry. Nihil noticed his tears. She replied: "The missionary told me tears are a reminder that we all come from the waters of life." James remained quiet but Nihil hugged him tightly as a way of thanking him for her life.

Every time they visited the island the strong feelings were experienced by Nihil. Once they left the spot the sensation seemed to leave. One time it did not die when they left the spot. Nihil simply thought the experience was unusual. The same experience happened three times. Finally Nihil said: "We are going to have our own child."

James was overjoyed. As the presence of the child became more obvious he began to feel a little guilty. He had been taught that a father and his daughter having a child is wrong. He began to wonder who is wrong me or Nihil? Are both of us wrong?

James spoke to several men on the island. They did not understand what James was saying. Finally James asked to meet with several of them together. Again none of them seemed to understand what law is. Finally one said: "We are simple people. We do not understand what law is. We live simply, share everything we have and do not try to tell anyone what he or she can do or not do."

James felt better but he still had some doubt. He decided to talk to Nihil. She told him: "You said our spirits are not bound by the same restrictions as our bodies. Our spirit is present in many different places at the same time. We need to be sensitive to that presence. Let us be sensitive to the spirit present in my body."

When the persons on the island heard about the child they built a huge bonfire, stood around it and sang a joyful song: "every child is a gift which reminds us we are bound together by love. We commit ourselves to love her."

Each person holds a twig from a tree on the island. Nihil lights her twig/torch from the fire and hands it to James. He lights the twig of the person next to him. Each person lights the twig of the next person until all twigs are lit. The joyous song continues: "we all share the light of this child. We will share her light with anyone we meet."

This song is repeated until all the twigs are lit. Nihil walks around the circle. Each person lays a hand on her baby. One of the leaders of the island stands in the center of the group and says: "We will share her light with anyone who comes to our island."

People of the island began building a shrine to Nihil and her baby. They built it at the shrine where Nihil had been conceived. They placed a series of stones in a large circle and said "This is the world in which we live." Inside the large circle they built a smaller circle. "This is where we live." In the center of that circle they placed two atones. "This is Nihil and James. They are part of our circle, also part of a bigger circle – the world in which we all live." When the child was born they placed a smaller stone between Nihil and James.

The natives built a huge bonfire. Nihil and James presented the child to each person so each person could touch the child who touched each of them in so many ways. The group sang another joyful song: "The fire is warmth and light. This child is a new light. Her presence warms our hearts. We know that her spirit will remain with us always. We are richer because of her spirit." A similar ritual was performed several nights. The final night the child was named. Several names were suggested. One person said: "She isl warmth and light, name her WALAWUA."

As she grew Walawua received so much love and attention from everyone she began to wonder who among them wore really her parents. She began asking others. Some said Nihil. Walawua asked Nihil who told her: "I am the one who carried you in my body for several months. James is the one who made it possible for me to carry you in my body and for you to have life."

Walawua did not understand what her mother was saying but Nihil continued: "Without the love and care everyone showed me and you, I would never have been able to bring you to life." After a pause Nihil continued: "Love all the persons on this island who helped bring you your life. There are also other persons who are not on this island who also helped me to give you life."

Walawua accepted her mother's answer. Eventually she wanted to meet some of the other persons who made her life possible. Nihil told her: "When you are a little older, we will help you understand."

The excitement caused by the birth of Walawua was so intense no one on the island noticed a large ship which sailed up to the island. One person was on the boat which had large equipment on it. The man on the ship recognized James. He also recognized Nihil.

James and the new arrival had been on a boat which shipwrecked on this island. They recalled their pleasant experience due to the welcoming attitude of the natives. They talked about discovering oil on the island. James told him: "I became close to Nihil and we gave birth to a child."

The newcomer replied; "I heard that you had a child but no one could find you. I would like to meet your child." Nihil brought Walawua to meet the visitor. She told Walawua: "You are going to meet a person, who in a small way, helped give you life.

Walawua hugged the man and said: "Thank you helping to give me life." The visitor was shocked by the story of Nihil. He said: "The persons I work for are involved in providing oil. We are running low on oil. There are not as many persons looking for oil. Our customers use oil in a different way. They need more oil. We wasted oil here and we need to get back the oil we wasted here."

His equipment was loaded on the island. It began to skim the water and deposited something in a large barrel on the ship. The visitor also cleaned up the dead fish to use to produce oil. The natives were happy, amazed, and fascinated. They were overjoyed their land was usable again. Walawua was especially interested in the project. She had been told the visitor was one of the persons who is part of the group who helped her have life.

There was a lot of excitement because of the growth of Walawua and the cleaning up of their island. Large ships were constantly passing by the island. Each had large plastic bags which seemed to be full. No one, including James, knew what they were or what they contained. Some natives asked where they came from or where they were going. Walawua wondered if the persons on the ships were part of the group of persons who helped her to be born.

Nihil and James also became interested in the ships, their cargo, where they came from, and where they were going. They decided to follow one of the incoming ships. James said he had to make a few repairs on his boat. It had not been used for a long time.

Walawua told them: "We are going to find some of the persons who made it possible for me to be born. We will be back." She added: "This will help all of us understand we do not live alone. We are part of a larger group of persons." She pointed to the shrine they built for her birth. "We are in a small circle which is all of us. There is a bigger circle which shows us we are part of a bigger group. This group helped me to be born. I want to find them."

The natives recalled the ceremony at the birth of Walawua. They realized she was not only expanding her circle, she was also expanding their circle.

As Walawusa, Nihil and James were leaving, all persons on the island gathered on the shore. They remembered something Nihil said of her wandering before she came to the island. They sang a joyful song: "We came from somewhere. When we leave there we bring something from that place and we leave something of our self. When we leave there we bring something of our self as well as something from wherever we have visited."

The natives presented the three departing persons with a long string tied in a circle and filled with knots. One person explained: "Each of us made a knot in the string. Keep it as a reminder of us. One part of the string can be opened so you can add persons you visit."

Nihil took the ring she was given, opened it and placed it on a ring she had been given when she left Alaska. She said: "The string I received in Alaska is a reminder that all of us are bound together with persons from other places. I place the ring you gave me on my own ring as a sign we who live on this earth are bound together with persons everywhere."

Nihil was sad and excited as she left the island. She remembered the sadness when she left other places. She touched her ring and the new ring she had just been given. She knew despite her sadness some force within her always prompted her to go on. She would eventually find what she wanted. The knots in the string reminded her to keep going

Walawua and James had different emotions than Nihil. Walawua was excited. She was going to new places and she would find new persons who were almost like parents. In their own way they had helped her to be born and become the person she is. James was thinking of all the times he had moved along these waters. He wondered what new experiences he would have. His life had changed so much. He also wondered about the plastic bags in the ships. He knew they did not carry oil. What did they contain? Where did they come from? Where are they going?

Each one was so engrossed in personal thought. They almost missed an island. He knew this is the first island they would see. He knew this was the island where he and Nihil met. Nihil also noticed the island where they had met. But the island seemed different. They took Walawua to see where they had met. They entered the island and stopped to pray for themselves and anyone who passed here. They also prayed that the land would not be abused.

They looked for oil derricks. There were none. In their place were large objects which seemed to come out of the ground. James had some idea what they were, but had never seen one. They walked further and saw a man pouring something into the object. James had worked with him. The man had recently been to their island and removed the oil. He was surprised and said: what are the three of you doing here?

Nihil said: "I am looking for the island where I met James."

Walawua said: "I am looking for persons like you who helped me to be born."

James said: "I am wondering what all the ships with large plastic bags are for? What is in them? Where did they come from? Where are they going?"

The man said: "I do not know where they are going. I am sure they are going different places – probably some port."

Walawua said: "I haven't seen any going to our island."

He laughed and said: "No! I don't think you will find any on your island.

"Don't they like us?"

"They probably don't even know you are there.

Then he turned to James and said: "They carry dead bodies. There is a war further up the water. Persons are being killed. Their dead bodies are being carried elsewhere."

Nihil and Walawua had no idea what he was talking about as they watched ships passing in an opposite direction to earlier ships. James wondered why he had been transporting oil from here to other places. Nihil was confused by all that she saw. She didn't know what to say. She looked at all the strange objects. She could not imagine what they were.

Nihil finally asked what the large objects were.

"Missles."

"What are they used for?"

"Fighting the war."

Walawua said: "LET'S GET OUT OF HERE!!!"

The experience on the oil island, the idea of war, was so troubling that no one spoke as they continued. James wondered what he had contributed to war. James suggested that they go back to their island. Walawua reacted strongly.

"NO!!!"

"Why???"

"I want to find others who helped me to be born."

"You won't find them further up!"

"We won't if we don't try."

Reluctantly James moved them on.

Soon Nihil shouted "The gold island!"

As they entered the island it seemed deserted. Nihil told Walawua and James:

"When I was in my mother's body I went looking for James" Walawua asked: "Was he there?"

"No!"

"What was there?"

"Gold."

"What is that?"

"It is used for money."

"What is money?"

"Something persons use to obtain what they need"

"Do we have any money at home?"

"No."

"Why don't we?"

"We are money to one another. We supply each other."

Walawua did not understand what her mother said. Her mother told her that she would understand later. That was all right with Walawua. As they were leaving the island they met a man. Nihil asked where the golf was.

"It has all been transferred to the next island"

Nihil remembers that island. It has a huge wall around it. Men with guns stand in front of the wall. There is a huge sign telling everyone not to come in. Nihil told Walawua they would not be able to get into the next island. James said he avoided that island when he delivered oil.

When they reached the next island, the wall was broken, there were no men with guns, no one was bringing in money or gold. There was one man cleaning up. Nihil asked:

"What are you doing?"

"Some gold was left behind."

"What are you going to do with it?"

"Send it to London with the rest of the gold."

Now Nihil wanted to go home when Walawua asked "Why?' Nihil told her about the large buildings which had big signs saying they were set up to help people in need. They did not answer any of my questions. I asked if they would help the persons in Alaska where the ice was melting and dangerous material was being released. They told me they sent money to the next bank to do that. When I went to that bank they said there were many places that needed help so they could not send help to Alaska. Walawua asked:

"Does anyone help them?"

"No."

"It sounds like all these islands are connected. Someone should be able to help them."

Nihil and James marveled at the child's wisdom. Both of them were asking the same questions. Nihil said: "I am happy we live on our island."

On the way to the next island Nihil asked the others to stop. She explained to them: "I do not know the exact spot but somewhere around here I was born. My mother died a very short time after I was born. A sailor took my mother and me to an island where she died. I lived on that island until a missionary took me to Alaska and London. On my way from London to our island I visited the island where I was raised. I took some soil from my mother's grave. I placed that soil near here as a sign that we are still united with one another and with the sea. Then Nihil said to Walawua:

"I brought soil from where you were born. Place that soil here. We are part of one another and of the sea even if we are separated." Walawua placed the soil and asked:

"If we are united to the sea may I bring sea water home?"

"Yes."

It was a short trip to the island where Nihil's mother is buried. The natives were so happy to see Nihil. They wondered who the other two persons were. Nihil introduced James and told how she finally found him on the island she first visited when she went searching for James.

Nihil and James placed Walawua between them. They all held hands. Nihil explained this is our daughter. Her name means warmth and light. The natives formed a circle with Nihil, Walawua, and James.

"You are all part of us." They cheered and Walwua said.

"My mother said others are part of my birth."

"We are and we are proud off it".

Nihil asked them to show Walawua her own mother's grave. The entire group walked to the grave. Walawua asked:

"May I add my name and my father's?"

"Yes, please do."

One of the natives brought a tool for writing and gave it to Walawua. She gave it to James and said: "You go first." Jame's hands were trembling as he wrote his name. When Walawua wrote, she added her name and drew lines from James and Nihil. Walawua drew a picture of the sun with its rays. She explained:

"I came from Nihil and James. My name means warmth and light which the sun gives us. The sun is a sign of me. The rays of the sun show all of you."

Nihil and James were amazed at the wisdom and creativity of their daughter. The natives could not create the sun, so they created a huge bonfire. One native said:

"The warmth and light of the sun is not enough, we need to make it present. So we create a bonfire."

Several natives had gone to the garden. They brought back some of the crops. They said:

"The warmth and light of the sun also gives us food."

The natives prepared a meal to celebrate Nihil's return and the additions to her family. The night was spent sharing stories of each of their lives. In the morning a native said:

"Have you come back to stay with us?"

Walawua said to her mother and father: "OH, CAN WE?"

"No we have other places we need to visit."

Walawua was disappointed but Nihil reminded her that the reason they left their island was to find other persons who were a part of her birth.

As they were leaving, one of the natives presented Walawua with a stone from the fire last evening.

"Remember to spread your warmth and light wherever you go. This stone from our fire is a reminder that wherever you spread it, you also spread our warmth and light."

Many tears were shed. Nihil told Walawua tears are a reminder we all share something in common. We were formed in water in our mother's body. No matter how different we may be, we have the same beginning. Abuse of our life, our earth comes when we forget how we were born.

As they approached London there were more large ships. The ones with plastic bags containing bodies sailed in the direction they were coming from. Others were going in the same direction they were heading. These had no plastic bags. These ships stopped at London. Walawua wondered what they were doing. Nihil remembered the big buildings she had visited. She saw the money and gold coming from the buildings and placed on the ships. She knew the money and gold were being shipped for a purpose. She did not know why they were being shipped or where they were going. Nihil wanted to leave London as soon as possible. Nihil was fearful but was willing to follow the money ships.

Next they saw a group of persons in tents. Nihil heard someone call her name. She wondered how anyone this far from home would know her name. As they came closer Nihil recognized persons she knew in Alaska. They were so happy to see one another, they simply enjoyed being together. Nihil introduced Walawua and James. Walawua is our child. Walawua asked them how they got here.

"Our ice melted and left dangerous and deadly material once it melted."

"We had dangerous material at home and a man came with a machine and cleaned it up."

"This dangerous material killed our fish."

"The man with the machine cleaned up our dead fish."

Persons from Alaska told of friends they knew who died from the waste. Other persons became seriously ill. Even when we breathe the air it could be dangerous.

Nihil told of here experiences with the banks in London.

"I asked if they could help you. They said there were many needs. They could not help all persons in need."

Walawua said: "Maybe the boats with money will help."

Walawua suggested they follow the boats.

"Maybe they don't know about the problems in Alaska. If we tell them about the problem, maybe they will send some of that money to help the persons in Alaska."

Persons from Alaska said that would not happen.

"Walawua said: "It won't happen if we don't try."

James was very interested in knowing where the money was going. He also realized his daughter had an inborn sense of what needed to be done. He convinced two of the persons from Alaska, Kimo and Nino, to come with them to find out where the money was going.

There were now five persons in James' tiny boat. They soon came to a very devastated area. Everything seemed to be dead. The ships with plastic bags were leaving there. The ships with money were unloading money and gold there.

Walawua wanted to go and tell the money persons about Alaska. Except for Walawua, no one wanted to go there. They moved a little closer. Men on the ship pointed guns at them and told them to go away.

"Just like the money and gold island." Nihil observed.

They realized they could not go any further. They saw a man standing on the shore. He seemed frightened.

"Do you need a ride?" Walawua asked.

"I've got a ship."

The group sailed to the shore. Part of the man's clothing was cut. There were wounds on his body. He seemed to be frightened. Walawua asked: "What is your name?"

"Joe."

"What happened to you?"

"I was in a war"

"What's a war?"

"It is persons fighting over land and money."

"My name is Walawua. It means warmth and light are with us always. If land is with us always why would persons want to fight over land?"

"There is money to be made in war."

"If land is destroyed what good is money? Are the money ships here to fix up the land?"

The man began to cry. Walawua said:

"Tears remind is that we are all born in water. When we cry, we show that all of us care for one another."

The persons in the boat marveled at Walawua's simplicity and wisdom. Joe invited them to go together on his ship. They began to talk about reasons wars are fought – greed, ignorance, fear, insecurity, anger, envy, pride, unwillingness to listen, unwillingness to care.

Walawua overheard their conversation and said:

"When we remember that water and land are with us always and we are supposed to take care of them there is no reason for war."

Joe realized he not only needed to join this group and re-form his life. He needed to begin pursuing life instead of death. He said:

"I am happy you allow me to join you. With a large ship we can take many others with us.'

They left in Joe's ship and reached the Alaska group's camping area. Kimo and Nino invited their group to come with Nihil's group. They all realized they had many things in common. They began to share stories with each other.

Joe told them about missiles which came over the land. They killed persons, devastated the land and then left.

Walawua asked: "Didn't they like the persons there?"

"They were afraid persons on the island would join another group that didn't think and act the way they did."

"You mean they lived so close to water and didn't know we all were born in water?"

"I guess they never thought about that."

"Are there some of your group who are still back where you picked us up?"

"Most of them left but a few are still there."

"Could be go back and tell them we all came from water?"

"I don't think they would listen."

"Maybe we could show them how all of us here are different but we all get along together."

Joe was impressed by the child's wisdom, He reflected on his own torment and that nothing good came of it. He paused and reflected on the death of so many persons. Finally he told Walawua:

"I sure wish you were right!. Unfortunately not too many persons think the way you do!"

Walawua said: "Who is on the island?

"There are the natives. They want to live in peace. Many of them were forced to leave their homo."

"Were you the one who forced them?"

"I was part of the group who forced them?"

"Didn't your group of persons like them?"

"We didn't even know them."

"Why would you want to harm persons you don't know?"

Joe was quiet. He had never asked that question. All he could think of was all the crops he had helped destroy. How his group was fighting another group. Neither of them had any claim to the land. He remembered how many of his friends were shipped away in plastic bags.

Joe remembered how many persons asked him to tell members of his family that he loved them. He did not even know how to reach his family or how he could have the courage to tell them. For the first time he realized that no matter how much we are different, war is one human being killing another human being.

Does anyone profit from war? Joe thought of all who made money from war, companies who sell the weapons we use, military persons who make a living from war.

-24-

Joe had no answer for Walawua. Their dialogue was so moving that everyone remained silent for several minutes. Finally Kimo spoke "We were not involved in any war. Our land was destroyed. Some persons were killed. Some, like us, have been forced to leave our land."

After a pause Kimo continued: "Low flying planes dropped something on our land. Men came in and began to dig into the ice. That is when persons began to die."

"They could be searching for oil. But that would not have caused persons to die!" Joe said.

"There were other men who came. They wore very heavy clothing. Their heads were covered with heavy masks. They dug up material from below the ice.

I saw those men in another place. They were not wearing any of the strange looking clothing. I heard them talking about something they called nuclear – whatever that is. One of them said it was under the ice and as the ice melted, there would be more."

Before they had a chance to finish their conversation they came near another island. Nihil seemed afraid. The sight of the two large buildings brought back very unpleasant memories of her first visit there. This time there were two persons standing on the shore not just one. Walawua was the first one to come off the ship.

"Hello! My name is Walawua, it means warmth and light are with us always."

The stranger was shocked but said:

"My name is Rob as in Robert."

Walawua introduced herself to the other person.

"My name is Frank."

"Do you work together?"

"Well, in a way." Rob said.

"How?"

"I make sure Frank has everything he needs so he can do his work"

As Walawua was talking to Frank and Rob the other members of the ship joined them. Kimo recognized Frank.

"Didn't I see you in Alaska?"

Frank wondered how he was recognized. His confusion was apparent. When he didn't answer Kimo said:

"I think I saw you where the ice was melting. You were wearing heavy strange looking clothes. You dug up something and put it in a strange looking container. I saw you later in a different place. You were talking to someone else and you talked about nuclear."

"Nuclear waste."

"If it is waste" Walawua said "why don't you use it again? At home we use all of our waste – human, animal, and plant waste. It is very helpful growing food."

"I don't think the waste we get would be helpful in growing food."

"If you would come to our island we could help you find some use for your waste."

Frank was amazed by the simplicity of Walawua. He did not want to go any deeper in this discussion. While they were there several ships stopped and picked up some money and a few small chips.

James met a man whom he had met on his trips to deliver oil. He asked:

"What are the chips for?

"The army implants them into soldiers in order to help them undergo extreme stress. Some are used to make a soldier appear to be dead so he may be ignored if he is shot, to help him go for long times without sleep, to help soldiers forget in case they are captured, and for other purposes."

"Couldn't these measures work against the army?"

"Yes! Sometimes they do."

Walawua said: "Let's go." Nihil agreed with her daughter.

As the group continued their journey Walawua said: "We started from our island so I could find persons who assisted in my birth. I see know that there also are persons who have hampered my birth."

"That's an important lesson to learn in life. Some persons never seem to learn that lesson" Nihil told her daughter.

In a short time Joe saw one of the ships carrying plastic bags tied up along the shore. He stopped the ship and pulled into a cove away from the main course of the sea. The other passengers on the ship wondered why. Joe said:

"Don't you notice movement in several of the bags? Everyone in those bags is not dead." Then several soldiers came out, removed the bags from the ship and opened them up. Live soldiers were in the bags. Some needed to be carried. Some seemed to be disoriented. All seemed to have some disability.

Joe followed the group of soldiers escorting the soldiers taken from the bags. He was careful enough to follow at a safe distance so he would not be seen. He saw the wounded soldiers brought into an area with a huge fence around it. He climbed a large tree with enough trees that he would not be seen. A small chip was taken from each soldier. They began to walk normally – just as James said, he thought

Their ship left quickly. No one wanted to be seen in that area. Joe and James exchanged stories about their particular experiences. Both of them were astounded that despite different life styles they had come to the almost identical conclusion that we are all related. It was a time for each of them to reflect on the meaning of their common journey. Although it took almost an hour to make this last part of the trip it seemed like only a few minutes before they arrived at the island where Nihil had lived.

The islanders were excited to see Nihil and her family. They were excited to see so many newcomers. One person said: "Every time you come to see us you bring a few more persons with you. It helps to be more aware of how we are all united."

"We all come from water." Walawua said.

The natives prepared a huge bonfire and a meal from the own garden. They sat around the bonfire. Walawua said:

"I went on this trip hoping to find persons who are part of my being born. Many of them are here with us now. I also found some persons who did not seem to care that we all came from water and are united by water. Some tried to use the water around them to harm other persons. No matter what they do we need to remember that we have to think of them as persons who also came from water."

Everyone was touched by Walawua's comments. Nihil showed the ring she was given by Kimo and her family. She passed the ring around for everyone to touch. She said:

"We are linked by this ring."

Nihil then took the open string she had been given by the persons on the island where she lives. She said:

"I was given this gift with a knot tied by each person on the island. I was asked to take this gift and place a knot for each person I met. I ask Kimo to take the gift and tie a knot and take it to each person to tie a knot in it. After all of us tie our knot we will leave the string untied because there are always more persons who need to be a part of our ring."

There were so many knots that another string needed to be added. Each person added to the string. The natives were interested in all the stories especially those of Kimo and her family. Nihil had already told them part of the story about the persons from Alaska. The visit was so interesting and exciting that the visitors stayed for several days.

It was a sad but joyful departure. Nihil spoke: "We shall come again to visit." A leader of the natives gave one of their members, Amicua, to Walawua with water from the sea. She said: "Here is water from our sea. The water and Amicua means we are bound together by the water of birth. Bring Amicua back to with a person from your island."

Amicua and Walawua immediately became close friends. They were able to share so many common experiences. Walawua told Amicua of her journey to find persons who helped her to be born she said:

"Of all the persons I met you are the most precious. Your family took care of my mother. A part of you and your family will always be a part of me." When the ship passed near the spot where Nihil was born, Walawua took a portion of the water and gave a portion to Kimo and her family as well as to Joe. She said: "All of you are part of our family."

They arrived by boat at the island of Nihil, James, and Walawua. Nihil took the sting with all its knots. She said: "The string you gave me is now much longer. We had to tie on an extra length of string because we met so many persons who are a part of us."

Nihil introduced Kimo and all the persons from Alaska who travelled with them. Each of them said a few words of greeting and thanks. Nihil introduced Joe who told of his conversion from thinking in terms of war to thinking about the unity of all persons and how war destroys that unity.

Then Walawua introduced Amicua and told everyone about Amicua. "She and I have so much in common. We have many common ancestors and experiences. The persons on Amicua's island sent her to us. We are to bring her back to the them send one of us to them"

Epilogue

The missionary who buried NIHIL'S mother and helped raise Nihil came back to check on Nihil and her re - discovered family. Nihil was so happy to see him. Nihil showed the missionary Walawua. "This is the child of James and me." Then Nihil, James and Walawua took the missionary on a tour of the island. The people of the island followed and sung a joyful song,

The missionary asked everyone to stand in a circle. He offered a prayer of thanksgiving. He invited Walawua to come into the center of the circle. He placed his hands on her and said: "Each new life that comes among us is a reminder that we all share the same life no matter how different we may be. No war or other human tragedy can change the fact we are one and called to take care of one another." Then Nihil, James, Kimo, Nino and her family and Joe stood in the center of the circle and song a song in the language of the people: "We all came from the waters of life. We all came to be because two persons loved each other. Life is dependent on that love. Water and love binds all persons together." Joe added in a solo: "No war, disagreement, or human tragedy can destroy our common beginning."